When Wisdom Arrives:

FROM IMAGINED UNWORTHINESS TO FREEDOM

ROSALYN ROURKE, MSW
ILLUSTRATED BY ADAM CAMPBELL

When Wisdom Arrives:
From Imagined Unworthiness to Freedom

Copyright

Printed in the United States of America

Hardcover ISBN: 978-1-960876-20-1
Paperback ISBN: 978-1-960876-21-8
Ebook ISBN: 978-1-960876-22-5
Library of Congress Control Number: 2023941610

Muse Literary
3319 N. Cicero Avenue
Chicago IL 60641-9998

When Wisdom Arrives: From Imagines Unworthiness to Freedom offers proven keys to move out of chronic unhappiness to contentment. After the fable, I share my own story in the Memoir Companion. When my daughter unexpectedly died at age 39, I traveled through profound grief to radical acceptance. I found that there is a way to release the fight in us, no matter what has happened.

You can receive the same transformation that the protagonist in the fable and I have experienced by applying what Wisdom teaches in the fable. I would love to continue our relationship and be there for your realizations and questions.

This QR code will guide you to bonus materials on my website where you will:

- Find meditations to guide you to connect with your "True I."
- Receive up-to-date, behind-the-scenes details about book tour events and happenings.
- Gain access to a free When Wisdom Arrives Book Club with me on Zoom.
- Have the opportunity to take an Unworthiness Quiz and receive a written and video guide to my training: Five Steps From Imagined Unworthiness to Living in Contentment Now.
- Receive a gift of *The Tulip and Tree*, a fable revealing a different way to view death, loss, grief and causeless joy.
- Gain admission to my free group: A New Paradigm for Grief.

- Get the link to join me for a free Glimpses of Awakening Class, where we'll apply the teaching from the book to your own life and find the opportunity of freedom now.

Access all of this and more here:

Or on my website at
www.rosalynrourke.com/when-wisdom-arrives-from-imagined-unworthiness-to-freedom/

To Phil and Ally:
This is for you both, for being my partners in the best and worst of times. Your love and support make all the difference.

To Marion:
I cannot imagine life without you. Your heartfelt support and loyalty have bolstered me throughout this journey.

To Melissa:
You have been my daughter, my teacher and my companion in laying down the ancestral trauma of imagined unworthiness. Thank you for all you have been to me.

INTRODUCTION

*"Out beyond ideas of wrongdoing and rightdoing,
there is a field. I'll meet you there.*

—Rumi

If thoughts and feelings were truth, we would call them facts. Yet many of us consistently treat our thoughts and feelings as truth, even when they tell us we're unworthy. Imagined unworthiness is often created by children to give them an imagined sense of control. Now, as adults, the tyranny of these hurtful thoughts and feelings torture us and create addictions and compulsive thinking. We create repetitive stories around our imagined unworthiness that loop again and again and become the source of our suffering.

We've been conditioned to try to fix our unworthiness in the outer world by focusing on improving ourselves through achievement, status, power, respect and body perfection. When our attempts to feel worthy have not been successful, we often draw dismal conclusions about ourselves. Our critical, judgmental thoughts flow in painful loops that pile on more hurt. Even when our seeking efforts are successful, the burst of worthiness from acquisitions and goals achieved is temporary. The high can appear to be a fix because we feel better. Until the high wears off. When the old thoughts and feelings of unworthiness return, the next seeking takes over. Suffering continues as we repeatedly try to fix the wrong things.

What if our value were not in question and our true worthiness has been inside all along, hidden in plain sight? From my 30 plus years as a psychotherapist, I believe we all long for the end of suffering and something more than transitory happiness. We have learned to focus on the future and the past in order to try to feel better now. But freedom from imagined unworthiness, and the exuberance, joy, acceptance and creativity that freedom brings, can only be found in the Now. Without our old looping thoughts and feelings and the narratives we add, we can experience a new moment where suffering ends and anything becomes possible. Freedom is about possibility.

This memoir-fable demonstrates a powerful way out of suffering and into freedom. In these pages, I provide a simple, specific strategy for how to know our worth by intervening in the old thinking-feeling patterns that cause psychological suffering. This book's simple protocol will help all of us who desire to discover freedom.

In the fable, we meet young Gem and her mother who believe a lie that their worth is in their body size. Gem's looping thoughts and feelings about her body and her worth cause her psychological suffering. With the help of a gentle, wise teacher, Gem learns a simple way to intervene in her hurtful thinking-feeling patterns. She discovers how to connect instead to her True "I," the deeper, gentler part of all of us. The True "I" never judges and can serve as a guide and life raft from upset to ease in living. Discovering her ever-present True "I" is life-changing for Gem, just as it can be for all of us. When we know our True "I," our worth is not in question and consistency and groundedness become our homebase.

I wrote this book to share how pain and suffering can transmute into freedom, because I've lived it. I had a similar experience to Gem's, when I moved out of suffering to freedom after the unexpected death of my daughter. My story in the Companion provides the backstory of how the teachings in this book came to me.

Most of us believe freedom has to be hard-won. If you share that belief that freedom is hard to find and sustain, I challenge you to apply the protocol shared in this book and see for yourself how quickly you can experience a break from psychological suffering. The gift of this book is to know that our old beliefs of unworthiness were imagined. It's a joy to know that freedom and even grief resilience are possible for everyone.

WHEN WISDOM ARRIVES: FROM IMAGINED UNWORTHINESS TO FREEDOM

Once there was a girl named Gem, who wondered why her mom scrunched her eyebrows at herself every time she looked in the mirror. One day, when Gem scrunched her eyebrows at her own reflection, an image of an old woman appeared in the mirror.

Gem: Who are you and where did you come from?

Wisdom: My name's Wisdom, and I come when people need another way to understand what is going on with their feelings and thoughts.

Gem: How do you know what's going on with people?

Wisdom: It is my job and my beloved purpose to visit people and make a heart connection with them.

Gem: What's a heart connection?

Wisdom: Have you ever started talking to someone and they understand you so deeply that you feel like you have always known them?

Gem: Not really. I don't really have any friends. I talk to myself and sometimes to Sissy. But she's younger and doesn't understand how I feel about things. She's skinny and can't understand what I go through.

Wisdom: I heard you ask the mirror why your mommy scrunches her eyebrows when she looks at herself. Gem, your question made me want to visit you. May I answer your question?

Gem: If you know the answer, *yes*, I want to hear!

BELIEVING THE "NOT GOOD ENOUGH" THOUGHT

Wisdom: Your Mommy thinks her body is not right.

Gem: But she's skinny like Sissy. I feel like she's frowning at me when she frowns at herself. Then, I feel icky.

Wisdom: Something is going on for you and your mother that went on between your mother and her mother before you.

Gem: What?

Wisdom: Your mommy and your grandma—

Gem: You mean my Oma?

Wisdom: Yes, your Oma. Your mommy and your grandma, Oma, plus your great grandmother, Oma's mother, all thought that they were not good enough. All of them focused their imagined unworthiness on each other's body parts: *My hips are too big* or *my daughter's stomach is getting scary big.*

Gem: Why did they do that?

Wisdom: When Oma grew up with your great grandmother, they had life-threatening problems, because they lived in Germany when the Nazis took over. You know about the Nazi government, right?

Gem: Yes, that must have been awful. I read about Anne Frank and she had to hide and could not go out and play or get enough food. And if they found her from her hiding place, she might have been killed or taken away.

Wisdom: I am so glad you know about those times. Oma was about your age when the Nazis were starting to restrict Jewish people, and she was no longer allowed to go to school.

Gem: Oh! I know Oma loved books. She was excited every time I told her about my school experiences. Oma wished she could have made things for the Science Fair and won the reading contest like I did.

Wisdom: Your Oma had to get a job when she was twelve.

Gem: That's one year older than I am now.

Wisdom: Yup. And Oma's mother thought Oma was chubby. She used to wake Oma up extra early to run around the streets, so that she could lose weight. Oma's sister Miriam got to sleep longer because she was not chubby.

Gem: That wasn't fair. And wasn't Oma's mother scared for her because of the Nazis?

Wisdom: Oma's mother was scared about the Nazis, and she needed to find a place for her worry. She placed her fear of the Nazis into her thoughts and feelings about her daughter's weight. It sounds odd to us, but in her own way she thought she was doing the right thing by helping her daughter get slim. Oma's mom thought if Oma was thinner, she'd be well-liked and safer, and Oma's mom wouldn't have to worry as much.

Gem: But why is Mommy frowning now? She doesn't have to worry about the Nazis.

Wisdom: You're right. Thankfully, she doesn't. But we often repeat what happened in our families. Babies are born loving beings, and they take in all experiences as love. So, when Oma was finally safe in America and had your mommy, she judged your mommy's weight, just like her mommy had done to her. And on some level, your mommy felt like that was love. Then she did the same to you.

Gem: So, when my mommy frowns at me, she's repeating what her mommy Oma did to her?

Wisdom: *(nods)* Yes.

Gem: No one actually says anything about my fat, but I feel like my mom is always looking at my fat tummy. I am sad that there is something wrong with me.

Wisdom: Gem, it must be hard to feel sad about your body.

Gem: Uh huh. Oma hated Mommy's body and that hurt Mommy. Why does Mommy hurt me the same way?

Wisdom: I do not think your mom is trying to hurt you. She learned something as a child and young people take in everything that happens. When children grow up, they often repeat both their sad and happy childhood moments without realizing it.

Gem: Well, when I grow up, I'm not going to do stuff to my children that hurts them, just because it happened to me.

Wisdom: I bet you will not repeat things like most people do, because you are so aware of what hurts and what you do not want to happen with your children.

Gem: I hope so.

Wisdom: If your mom was alright with your size, how would you know?

Gem: I would love for her to stop wanting me to be different. I think her eyes would smile when she looked at me, and she would not scrunch her brows and look at my belly. It hurts because I can't seem to get my body to look the way she wants.

Wisdom: You are pretty sure you know what your mom is thinking. You have a lot of feelings about your own body, and I am wondering if you ever get confused about who is thinking what.

Gem: I get confused a lot. Even when my mom is not around. I wish for a different body and almost wish I could be a different person. Other kids seem to be at ease with themselves in class, or at lunch, or in sports. I have a hard time, and I feel sad and scared a lot.

Wisdom: Could we talk more about your sadness and fear and your thoughts about wanting to be different? It might help you to know more about the nature of feelings and thoughts.

Gem: Okay.

Wisdom: Good. Knowing the *truth* about thoughts and feelings can be a great gift.

THE NATURE OF FEELINGS AND THOUGHTS

Wisdom: Feelings and thoughts are not necessarily true. They may not even be logical to the one thinking of them. Feelings and thoughts can change from moment to moment. They are so changeable; we cannot hold them as *truth*.

Gem: What do you mean by *truth*?

Wisdom: If you are interested, I am going to teach you some big *truths* about thoughts and feelings that can lead you to great happiness.

Gem: I would love to be happy. Yes, teach me if you can, because I do not see what my thoughts and feelings have to do with my happiness.

Wisdom: I will show you which kinds of thoughts to trust in and which thoughts actually lead to more hurt and unhappiness.

Gem: If you're telling me my thoughts and feelings aren't true and I can't believe them, it feels like I am losing something, not getting a gift. On top of being too fat, now my feelings and thoughts don't matter? Where is the gift in that? I feel even worse.

Wisdom: Oh, I love how honest you are Gem. Let me explain.

Oma's mommy's thought weight was their family's problem. Those thoughts were untrue. They were in danger from the Nazis.

Gem: Yeah, it didn't make sense to have Oma running around the streets to lose weight when her life was in danger.

Wisdom: I agree, it didn't make sense. And when Oma grew up and had similar thoughts about your mommy's body, Oma's behavior hurt your mommy's feelings.

Gem: It hurts me to even think about all of that.

Wisdom: I understand why it hurts. Did you know that thoughts and feelings can be contagious even if they are not true, because we are all connected. For example, you may start thinking what your mommy thinks, even if it is illogical, or unfair, hurtful and not true.

Gem: I never imagined thoughts as contagious. You mean both good thoughts and bad thoughts spread?

Wisdom: Yes. I prefer not to call them good or bad, because then we fight with the thoughts that we call bad. We start to think we are bad for having those thoughts. We often end up judging ourselves harshly for those thoughts.

Gem: If we don't call them good and bad, what do we do with them?

WELCOME ALL THOUGHTS & DROP THE ROPE!

Wisdom: We welcome or allow them all without interacting or getting involved with the thought.

Gem: Now I think you might be nuts. You welcome even mean and nasty thoughts?

Wisdom: We wouldn't judge the thought as mean and nasty. We would notice the harshness and leave it alone. It would be a new policy of not touching some thoughts, because they are hurtful or not helpful.

Gem: I think I get it.

Wisdom: Let me show you this card I carry around because people of all ages need it.

The person in the picture is struggling with their thoughts and feelings about "what is" happening in their lives. When we fight with "what is," no matter "what is," we lose. Look at the person's face. While they fight "what is," the person is struggling. When we fight, we seem not to know that another way is possible. Ease, grace and strength are available the second we drop the rope.

Gem: Wisdom, What am I in a tug- of- war with?

Wisdom: When you have thoughts about your body size and what your mother is thinking about your size, you're tugging on the rope and you feel alone, right? Many of us forget that others have their secret problems that they're struggling with too. When you drop the rope, everything changes.

Gem: What changes?

Wisdom: When we drop the rope and the fighting is over, there is a new moment. Now, anything can happen. In the Now, we can experience life as new without past or future thinking which can drag us back to struggling and picking up the rope again.

Gem: If we don't try to stop or fight our thoughts, how do we keep thoughts from hurting us?

Wisdom: Everyone desires to stop thoughts that hurt. But trying to stop thoughts that hurt is the same as playing tug-of-war with them. How has it worked to fight your thoughts about your mommy's feelings toward your weight?

Gem: It feels worse and worse and I get nowhere, except feeling sad.

Wisdom: What we believe about the thought we just had is important, because we can change our mind about what we believe.

Gem: I have no idea what you are talking about.

Wisdom: Let me give you an example. Your size is your size. But your feelings and thoughts about your size are "what is" hurting you, not your actual size. If you had a thought that you are too smart for this world, would it hurt you?

Gem: No, because I would know I can't be too smart. Are you saying I could be the same weight and feel differently?

Wisdom: Yes, Gem, just like you could know that whatever intelligence you have is fine, so you could know that whatever body type you have at the moment is also fine.

Gem: Wow, it would be amazing to feel fine!

Wisdom: Gentle Listening might be just your ticket for fineness!

Gem: I never heard of Gentle Listening.

Wisdom: Gentle Listening is simply listening to our thoughts without judging them. Then we can notice if the thought is hurtful or helpful, or just neutral. We can do this same kind of Gentle Listening with all our thoughts, feelings and perceptions.

Gem: When I say, "I am so fat," it is definitely not neutral. I think about what I ate. Usually, I end up feeling like I should not have eaten all that cake.

Wisdom: Then what happens?

Gem: I go to the mirror and I already see the cake on my butt. I know it would take at least a few hours to get there, but I actually think I can see it there right away.

Wisdom: Which of those thoughts hurt?

Gem: All of them.

Wisdom: When you mentioned you would see the cake already on your butt, that's actually imagination, isn't it?

Gem: I guess that was my imagination.

Wisdom: We humans have great imaginations and we make things up without realizing it. Imaginations are great for painting and creative writing, but imaginations can distract us from "what is" true. And our imaginations can make up hurtful thoughts.

Gem: Really? I never thought my imagination could hurt me. When I think I'm fat and then see a cake on my butt, I know I feel upset. But I didn't realize I was hurting myself. I never thought I had a part in what happens in my mind.

Wisdom: Would you like to feel more steady and content about yourself?

Gem: You mean like steady on a bike, where you don't tip over, even when you hit a rock?

Wisdom: Oh, that is such a great way to explain the gift of allowing "what is." Gem, you just described the way you sometimes add on to your first thought of, *I am so fat.* When you join with the first thought by adding on more scary ideas, like you did when you looked in the mirror and imagined the cake you ate making your body bigger, how do you end up feeling?

Gem: I feel sick to my stomach, because of the food I ate that I promised not to eat, plus all the yelling in my mind.

Wisdom: Do you know why promises do not work?

Gem: Why?

Wisdom: Because minds are not logical the way a computer is. If you give a computer a command like **delete**, what happens? Instructions are followed and the text is deleted. Computers follow our commands; they don't lead on their own. But our minds often take over, bringing up random thoughts and connections that might hurt even more.

Gem: Like my thought about cake landing on my butt right after I swallowed it?

Wisdom: Exactly.

Gem: I thought I could count on my thoughts to help me. I think I've been taught that thinking makes the difference. I've heard adults say, "Think before you act."

Wisdom: Both thoughts and feelings are just a moment. And thoughts can say opposite things from moment to moment.

Could you feel on top of the world winning a game with Sissy and tell yourself how good your skills are and the next moment see your mom and wonder if she is thinking about your body? Do you go up and down like that?

Gem: Yes, it happens that way a lot. I can feel great about my homework and my mom comes in to say goodnight and I feel like she is looking through my robe and my nightgown at my tummy and I tell myself, *Mommy hates me.*

Wisdom: What if you were able to notice the thought about your mom looking at your tummy, without adding on about your mom hating you?

Gem: Do I just say *no* when I start adding on?

Wisdom: If you let that first thought or feeling go without adding on, science says it will disappear within ninety seconds.

Gem: Ninety seconds sounds like nothing. Let's count it.

Wisdom: Okay, here we go!

Gem: Ninety seconds is a lot longer than I imagined. Is ignoring the feeling or thought all I need to do?

Wisdom: Yes and no. We are not pretending the thought or feeling did not happen. Pretending does not work. But, if we acknowledge that thoughts or feelings happened without adding on, they become like passing clouds. We watch them and decide on the spot if they are one or the other: old hurtful thoughts and feelings like *I'm so fat* or neutral ones like *It's time to hand in my math homework.*

Gem: I can tell the difference on the spot between *You're so fat* and *It's time to hand in your math.*

Wisdom: Of course you can, and it is that easy to let go of struggling once we know we don't have to follow or add on to a hurtful thought or feeling just because we heard it, or felt it.

Gem: Do I have to do something to the hurtful thought?

Wisdom: All you have to do is notice it. You do not need to fix it. Just do not add to it and another thought or feeling will replace it in less than ninety seconds.

Gem: Are you really saying that I don't have to fix the mean thoughts by making them more neutral?

Wisdom: Yes, that is the gift of learning to notice the difference between helpful thoughts and feelings and those that are unhelpful. You do not need to be a fixer. When the mean thoughts get less attention or add-ons, they seem to lessen in importance.

Gem: Is it like, if the main people on my TV show get fewer lines, they might not stay the main characters?

Wisdom: Yes, exactly!

THOUGHTS MAY NOT BE TRUE, BUT THEY CAN BE STUCK ON REPEAT ANYWAY!

Wisdom: Most thoughts and feelings are not said just once. Those that repeat can reveal what we believe.

Gem: Is it our beliefs that keep us playing tug-of-war like the person on the card you carry?

Wisdom: You've got it. Beliefs are just our opinions, otherwise we would call them facts, or the *truth*.

Gem: Oh, so this goes back to what you said, that not all our thoughts are *truth*, right?

Wisdom: Yes! If you knew your thoughts were not true, how would it change *I am not good enough, because of extra weight?*

Gem: Oh, Wisdom, if I could believe that thought was false, I would already be happy. I have the same thought over and over and it's very convincing when that's all I hear. You said they last ninety seconds, but mine sometimes last all day.

Wisdom: [*chuckling*] I think in the past, you might not have noticed how you were adding to the first thought, is that right?

Gem: Yup, it seemed like I was receiving the *truth* all day. Now I see I was hurting myself with my own thinking.

Wisdom: We call repeating words like "I'm so fat" over and over to ourselves a "looping" habit, because the thoughts go round and round like a loop of yarn.

Gem: Oh, I play a string game that's all about the loop. I wouldn't be able to play that game if I didn't have a loop. Do thoughts and feeling habits depend on the loop?

Wisdom: I will have to remember that explanation. Gem, it is so accurate. When you have looping thoughts about your body fat, do they ever end up with you feeling content or joyous, or even okay?

Gem: Never, my loops are around Mommy not liking me because I don't look right. Each time it ends with me really sad.

Wisdom: Yes. When we are stuck in our looping hurtful thoughts, they always end up the same way for us. And even when the feelings and thoughts hurt, they can still become a repetitive pattern in us.

Gem: I always thought my thoughts were the *truth*. What's a thought pattern?

Wisdom: If you had the thought: *Mommy thinks I am fat,* that might be a common thought pattern, right?

Gem: Yup, I hear that thought a lot.

Wisdom: But if you heard some guidance that said, *You are okay just the way you are, let that thought go,* would you recognize that thought as outside your usual pattern?

Gem: Do you mean I could actually think thoughts like that? Yes, I would definitely notice a thought like that one!

Wisdom: What if that was a real statement coming from a deeper part of you than the one you are used to listening to? I call that deeper part, our True "I." My goal is to help you discover your True "I," which has nothing to do with weight.

Gem: There's a deeper part of me?

Wisdom: Yes. Would you be interested in knowing the You that never changes and lacks nothing?

Gem: Wisdom, it is weird that you said lack. I say that word to myself a lot. I lack thinness, which some people get and I don't. I feel the lack of friends and what it takes to be acceptable.

Wisdom: Then getting to know your innermost You that knows you are acceptable in every way and truly lacks nothing will be fulfilling your heart's desire, right?

ON THE WAY TO FINDING
THE TRUE "I"

Gem: If this True "I" is in me, definitely bring her out!

Wisdom: Gem, recognizing our True "I" is an inside awareness that each person can only experience for themselves. But I can show you ways to find your True "I." Let's play a game, so I can show you what I mean. The game's called Future Pulling, and in this game, you get to imagine a new future, but that future is right Now. Let's pretend you're on your favorite gaming website and in this Now you have friends you are playing with. Future Pulling is a way to use our imaginations to help us, rather than hurt us.

Gem: Yay, I like games.

Wisdom: Here are the rules. You just start talking about what you really want as though you already have it. In the game, we don't explain anything ahead. For example, you pretend you are already having fun playing video games with your new friends.

Gem: Should I just start?

Wisdom: Yes.

Gem: Well, I love having so many people to play with online. I invited three people and they **clicked "yes"** right away. These friends have the skill to play the hard games I like. I'm having a blast. We're laughing so hard that I forgot to have my snack after school. Mommy called me for dinner, but I didn't want to stop playing. This is a dream come true for me.

Wisdom: I stopped by your room and you did not even see me. I heard you laughing and giggling and screaming about the game. I could not believe how I started laughing and saying, "Go for it," even though I did not understand the game. Thank you, Gem, for showing me what pure joy looks like in you.

Gem: That felt real. Now I know what it is like to have fun with cool people who are gamers like me.

Wisdom: How come in Future Pulling you could invite people into the game and you could not before?

THE POWER OF OUR THOUGHTS

Gem: The only difference, I think, are my thoughts. Before, I was sure no one would want to play with me, except Sissy. In the game, I expected to have friends because the rule of your game is you can have everything you want, right?

Wisdom: Yes, exactly. In the Future Pulling game, we are stepping into our future, but we're doing it in the Now. Do you think that what you believe ahead of time could make a difference in having real friends online?

Gem: Maybe?

Wisdom: Why haven't you hit **"accept"** to join with the kids who invite you to play online?

Gem: I get scared when I picture them wanting to meet me outside the game and chat. Then they would see how I look and not want to be my friend.

Wisdom: When you think of having a friend, what are the qualities you would like in them?

Gem: I would like a person I could tell anything to and they would not blab. Also, someone who would stick up for me, if people were being mean to me. I like funny, smart people because I like to laugh and figure out life by talking with others.

Wisdom: Interesting, you didn't say you were looking for a tall or short person with dark or light hair that was skinny or fat.

Gem: Do you think my idea of what kids want was just one of those hurting thoughts that I should leave alone?

Wisdom: Uh huh!

Gem: What if I go online now for real? I want to see what might happen if I just say *yes* when online kids ask to play. I've never clicked *accept* before. If I don't believe my thought, *Do not accept,* I might actually do the opposite of that thought and

click accept.

A REALIZATION HAPPENS FOR GEM

Gem clicks on a real gaming link on the computer.

Gem: "Steven the Winner" wants to play. I am going to see if I can beat him.

Wisdom: I'll come back and see you later. Have fun.
Wisdom: Gem, what happened?

Gem: I had so much fun online, first with "Steven the Winner" and then when his friend "Bob the Boss" joined us. It didn't matter that we didn't know each other. We just played the game. It wasn't awkward, there were no questions. But then Mom called and all it took was her looking at my body for me to fall back down from the fun zone.

Wisdom: What did you tell yourself your mom's look meant?

Gem: I am fat and not good enough for her to love me, like she does Sissy. She doesn't look over Sissy's body the way she looks at mine.

Wisdom: When you were playing, what size was your body?

Gem: Huh, no size.

Wisdom: Exactly. Were you happy the whole time you were playing, or only when you were winning?

Gem: I felt okay the whole time.

Winning and losing were both good. Just playing was fun. When I played with the guys, it was like I was no weight, because I had no thoughts or feelings about my body.

Wisdom: You just had what I would call a Realization. You've discovered the feeling of aliveness and calm, an okayness that is found in the background of thoughts, feelings, perceptions and judgments. Your discovery of okayness, my darling Gem, is what I call the True "I." And where were all your worries?

Gem: Oh my God, my worries were gone. I didn't realize it. Everything changed for me, but my body did not change. I can't believe it.

Wisdom: We have been taught to believe we have to change the outer world to feel better. When you were in your fun zone, how did you feel about yourself?

Gem: I was so okay. It was the best because I wasn't worried or hating myself. I actually felt kind of free. It's like I was in a Freedom Zone.

Wisdom: Wow, the Freedom Zone is amazing, right? You did not have to struggle to get free, you seemed to merely turn your attention away from your regular focus on your body thoughts. Then what has always been present, your True "I," was allowed to shine through as freedom.

Gem: I liked that I did not have to fight any feelings or thoughts. Now I think I see how to get to the Freedom Zone; it seems that not fighting my thoughts leads me to my okayness. With okayness came a kind of joy, but for no reason. Am I feeling better because I stopped struggling with my thoughts about being too fat?

Wisdom: Yes, you let go of the tug-of-war about your body size. And in letting go of the tug-of-war, you opened the door for you to notice your True "I." You discovered your True "I" when you became aware of your okayness that was not tied to your looping thoughts. Earlier, we played a game imagining the future. How about now we play a backwards game?

Gem: Your games are fun. What are the rules?

Wisdom: I ask you a few questions and you use your memory to answer.

Gem: Okay, that sounds easy.

FINDING THE TRUE "I"

Wisdom: When you were five, you wanted different things and you had different thoughts and feelings than you do now, right?

Gem: Yes.

Wisdom: When you were five, did you feel like the same you that you are now?

Gem: Oh yes. When I was five, I was the same. Except now I look different, and of course I don't take Sissy's things anymore.

Wisdom: You are doing a great job getting into the game. Next, when you were eight, did you wish for different things and have different experiences than when you were five?

Gem: Yep, I did.

Wisdom: Did you have different kinds of thoughts and feelings from when you were five years old and then when you were eight years old and now at eleven?

Gem: Yes, very different.

Wisdom: But, remembering back, have you always felt like the same you?

Gem: Yes, it is like I was a different person on the outside and in my thoughts, but in another way, I am exactly the same. How can that be true?

Wisdom: That "I" is your True "I." It is always with you and never changes with your different ages or body form or thoughts or feelings. But, because it doesn't have a physical form, it can be hard to understand. It doesn't have a physical form because it's not limited. That's how the True "I" can be with you as you change and grow in life, and all the while you stay you.

Gem: I said I am the same "I" at all my different ages, but who is the person who gets different grades and reads a book and takes ballet. I didn't do ballet when I was five.

Wisdom: Great question. Let's call the outer self that seems to change the "Me."

Gem: Are you saying there are two of me?

Wisdom: Haha, that would be silly. It is more like this: You have roles in your life—like being a student at school or a sister at home—that look and feel different from your True "I." But they are all one, they only look and feel different. The True "I" is a deeper

part of you that you learned about when you took your focus away from your hurting thoughts and got to experience your okayness.

Gem: Is it my "me" that sometimes feels hurt and upset?

Wisdom: Yes, because the "me" takes things personally and the True "I" does not. When it's raining, we are clear that the rain has no effect on who we are. But if something else happens in the outside world that we interpret as personal, then we might conclude that we are worthy or unworthy depending on how the event went. For example, if someone didn't know the answer to a math problem when their teacher asked, they might confuse not knowing with their worth inside. It's just another confusion people share because we teach people that they are their thoughts, their feelings, their bodies and what they do.

Gem: That's a lot. I didn't get all of that. Are you saying that if I don't know the answer to the math problem, even though I feel embarrassed, it has nothing to do with my True "I."

Wisdom: If you remember your True "I," the embarrassment will fade. The 'me' feels embarrassed, but the True "I" always knows your okayness.

Gem: How can I remember my True "I"?

Wisdom: Your "I" is always there in the background. Your True "I" doesn't really have a gender, but I will call her *she* for our discussion. When you are ready to find her and bring her to the foreground of your attention, she will always be there for you, shining bright. She is steady like the bike that works even when it goes over a rock. And she never judges, she always allows what has already happened, without a struggle.

Gem: I like my True "I." She is loyal like what I said I want in a friend.

Wisdom: And she does not have opinions on bodies or anything else.

Gem: I remember when I stopped thinking about my body size and played games, I felt free.

Wisdom: Whenever you pause from your thoughts and feelings, you can change your focus to your True "I." A different experience becomes possible in the next moment.

Gem: When I was in the Freedom Zone gaming, you said I found my aliveness. That was my True "I," right? And I had no particular body size and I was happy just playing.

Wisdom: Exactly. That was your True "I."

Gem: So, would you say my Freedom Zone is my True "I" out playing in the world?

Wisdom: Gem, you amaze me. You got what I came to teach you.

Gem: When I don't think about my body, I am fine.

But, I can't always game to get out of thinking about my body.

Wisdom: Gem, you said that when you are not focused on your body, you are fine. Holding on to this okayness is not about avoiding your body thoughts and feelings. It's about knowing the True "I" that is more permanent than your body.

Gem: Huh?

Wisdom: Since your True "I" has no physical form, it is not limited like a body. Bodies are limited because we are born and we will die. But the "I" has no limits.

Gem: You mean like a superhero?

Wisdom: Yes, how do you think writers imagined their superheroes?

Gem: Because the powers are in their "I"?

OKAYNESS

Wisdom: *Yes*, the greatest power is to know the secret to okayness: where and how to find it.

Gem: I get that okayness and my True "I" are not in a place. You know, Wisdom, it's like okayness and freedom found me when we played your games.

Wisdom: And that's because they have always been there. Remember you took your focus off what your mommy's thinking and off your body thoughts.

Gem: Oh! Wow! Did freedom come because I switched my focus to the background?

Wisdom: Yes, by letting go of your focus on the outside—like how many friends you have, or the form of your body—your okayness showed up. It is always there, but the outer world can distract our attention and hide the True "I."

Gem: I hear my mom calling me. Should I go and see what she wants?

Wisdom: Yes, for sure.

Gem: I am scared. Caring about what my mom thinks has always taken me down.

Wisdom: Be yourself. Trust what you have learned. Remember your okayness and you are good to go! I will wait to hear how it goes.

Gem: Ok, bye. *Mom, where are you?*

Mom: *In the laundry room.*

Gem: How was your day?

Mom: I guess it was okay.

Gem: Want me to help fold?

Mom: Sure, that's sweet of you.

Gem: You look a little sad, is something wrong?

Mom: Well, I had a meeting with Sissy's teacher and I'm a little worried. The teacher says Sissy doesn't participate in class discussions.

Gem: Mom, have you forgotten about Sissy's okayness?

Mom: Her okayness? What are you talking about?

Gem: Well, I am just learning that we are all okay underneath. Don't you think that's true?

Mom: Hm, I've never thought about it that way.

Gem: Everyone has problems sometimes out in the world. But that doesn't change their okayness, right?

Mom: Wow, I have never stopped to think about our okayness underneath problems.

Gem: When we remember our okayness, the problems seem to disappear.

Mom: Gem, you are right. If I remember Sissy is okay, then maybe I won't be worried. And maybe it wouldn't even be a problem that Sissy doesn't speak out in class.

Gem: Maybe it isn't the right time or place for her to talk?

Mom: You are so smart. I love chatting with you. And I love your way of seeing the world. I've been missing you. I've been distracted trying to decide if I should change jobs.

Gem: Ask your okayness what to do. You'll know.

Mom: Haha! Ask my okayness and trust the answer? You are funny and brilliant, Gem. Thank you for that help.

Gem: Thank you, Mommy.

Gem: Wisdom, you won't believe what happened. I just helped Mommy with her problems by telling her about trusting her okayness. I didn't tell her about you or the "I" and the "me," but I could feel how much Mommy loves me. I love her. I almost feel like I don't remember the problems we had. I know I could remember, but that is exactly what you have taught me <u>not</u> to do, right?

Wisdom: You are so wise, my little one. How wonderful that you did not bring your old story back into the Now. If you keep your interest focused on everyone's okayness, you will stay in okayness. Still, things might happen that you might not choose, but if you don't fight with what happens, all can be well inside you.

Gem: I'm not sad anymore. I'm excited to play my life as an okayness game.

Wisdom: Gem, I love you, and now you love you and you know that your mommy has always loved you. Would you care if someone at school said they didn't like you?

Gem: I would feel bad for them, because I would know they had not found their okayness yet.

Wisdom: You are my little wise friend. Can I call on you, the next time I go to a girl who needs help with her thoughts and feelings?

Gem: Oh, that would be fun. How will I get there?

Wisdom: I will surprise you when it is time for our first adventure together.

Gem: Are you leaving now?

Wisdom: Yes, but you'll always have me with you in your heart and if you ever need me, call for me, and I'll be there.

Gem: These are happy tears, Wisdom. Thank you for what you've given me.

Wisdom: You are welcome. Remember, my love is always with you, dear one. Bye for now.

MEMOIR COMPANION: MY STORY

At 12 years old, I weighed 212 pounds and the numbers were quickly climbing. I babysat, so I had money to buy sweets and extra lunches. Mostly I ate in secret. One day, feeling brave, I went to Ray's, the corner soda fountain store in my hometown in the Bronx, sat down on a stool and ordered a hot fudge sundae. When Ray arrived with a sundae dish dripping with chocolate and piled high with crunchy nuts and pillows of whipped cream, I was ecstatic. I took out my quarters and felt like a million bucks. *This is what it's like to be a skinny person and eat in front of everyone.* That night my mother said, "I heard you bought a chocolate sundae at Ray's."

I was still standing, but I felt like I had dropped to the floor.

Why had Ray betrayed me and joined my mother in trapping me? I already felt trapped in my mind from my thoughts and feelings that I was unlovable because of my size. That hot fudge sundae at Ray's was 63 years ago and the memory of being caught is still present. I was tied to my mother over our body sizes for years to come.

When I was 7 years old, my mom picked me up from school early to go with her to my first diet clinic. I don't remember that food plan, but I do remember that after we got weighed in, we ate grilled cheese sandwiches and skim milk with vanilla that my mother carried in her purse. Eating lunch out with only Mom was special. But being fat mostly meant we didn't deserve to eat food, especially good food. Diet food was alright. If we did get to eat something yummy like grilled cheese, we had to count it in a system or promise to eat less the rest of the day; or more days, depending on the severity of the punishment. My Sissy did not have to live by our fat rules, because she was skinny.

My preoccupations with food and body size were much like Gem's in our fable. Just like Gem, I was hurting. My mom couldn't stop trying to "help" me, just as the past mothers in three generations behind me and behind Gem could't stop "trying to help" their daughters. Little did I know then that I was destined to repeat all the so-called helping with my daughter Melissa, making us now three-plus generations of mothers and daughters in conflict and obsession over body size.

I had two daughters. I singled out Melissa, my second born, to worry about, just as my mom had with me. Melissa was a robust, happy child and when she started to have a chubby stomach, I started worrying and restricting her food. I was fooling no one, least of all Melissa. By the time I had Melissa, I had been slim for years, but I was not relaxed about being able to stay that way. I still believed my worthiness or unworthiness was 100% dependent on my size. Being 212 pounds as a child was not fun: I was bullied at school and felt excluded. I wanted Melissa to be included and enjoy a childhood different from mine.

I had been a psychotherapist for five years before Melissa was born. As she grew up and grew in girth, the pull to repeat generations of mothers focusing on one daughter's weight was stronger than my knowledge. I began studying A Course in

Miracles, a spiritual system of psychological nonviolence. I went to India and learned about Non-Duality. I became an eating disorder expert. None of this expansive learning stopped the dynamics from my ancestry.

When Melissa became an adult, we talked about the harm I'd caused by treating her differently and worrying about her size. I acknowledged my wrongdoing. I still saw hurt in her eyes. I did better as the years went on, but I still focused my worry on her. In 1995, I had my first transformation with food. I studied non-dieting and brought in all the previously forbidden foods into the house in large quantities. My commitment to myself and to the program was that if the quantities went halfway down, I would replace the supplies. I was done with restricting foods and with outsiders' rules governing my food.

And I was willing to gain weight if it helped me with food obsession and my relationship with Melissa. Having my house filled with formerly forbidden food cured my binge eating and most of my good-bad ideas about food. Most importantly, I was cured of the belief that I could not be trusted with certain foods. At that time, I was still attempting to influence Melissa's relationship with food, now from the non-dieting viewpoint. I wanted to undo the restrictive ways I'd taught her. I think she was surprised to see me eat foods I had previously not allowed.

For the first time in my life, I was having conversations with my body about what it would like to eat. It took a while for me to know that I am actually free to eat chocolate or potatoes, or not eat them. I was stunned to learn that healthy eating is sometimes getting too much of something and other times wishing I had more. Flexibility with food, without rules, felt like a miracle. Did I gain some weight when I was learning? Yes. The miracle was that too was okay. Letting go of the restrictive mindset, morphed into a generally more relaxed phase of life.

In 2012, I retired from my profession as a psychotherapist with a very rewarding practice and moved from Seattle to Florida for winters. Melissa was part of this new and exciting part of life. I apologized to Melissa for not teaching her about the joys of life. I told Melissa I didn't think I gave her permission to have a joyful life. I realized that as an adult, I would think of a problem before I called my mother, so we could relate about the problem. More than once, Melissa and I talked about our past and my deep regret about living out generations of obsession about food, body and weight with her. I told her I would like to change this with her. She knew exactly what I meant.

Melissa had to go on her own journey with food, and she did. She found a coach and lost 100 pounds, but still struggled with weight on and off after that time. While things with Melissa improved when I stopped restricting food, I still held some opinions about how Melissa was eating and frequently worried about her.

Everything changed after a trip to Ireland in 2017. I traveled with my husband and some dear friends to Kilkenny. My friend Maureen figured out how we could schedule a personal consultation with the Irish mystic, Lorna Byrne. It turned out that Lorna's effect on me was quite like what happened to Gem and her mother. Lorna said, *"You must stop worrying about Melissa!"* Lorna is a gentle, mild-mannered, soft-spoken person. Even though she was not actually yelling, I heard it as *"Stooooppppp!"*

Lorna did not tell me how to stop worrying. But from years of watching my thoughts from my A Course in Miracles and Non-Duality training, I could immediately see which thoughts were worry and which thoughts were neutral. Finally, it seemed I was ready to let the worry thoughts pass by, without joining in. With 100% of my heart available for this venture, I was all in. If a thought of worry about Melissa happened, I did not touch it. My husband Phil and I stopped discussing Melissa in any way that included thoughts of worry. I came to understand that by pulling back my interaction with the hurtful pattern of worrying about Melissa, my True "I" became available. More and more, there was a calm and peaceful place that was available within me, especially for Melissa.

Once I lessened my interest in worrying thoughts, the loops lost their attraction. The compulsion to think about Melissa in a worrying way dropped off. It was similar to letting go of the pulling in the tug-of-war card that Wisdom shows Gem. Once I dropped my side of the rope, the back-and-forth tugging was over. A new playing field emerged with Melissa. We seemed to be living more in the present. Our interests widened; we shared our work, concerts, visits to spas, lunches out, shopping, walking, house decorating. When the focus on food and body weight stopped, worrying and judgment were lifted.

Through Lorna, I had had my own experience with a Wisdom character appearing in my life to offer an intervention for the stuck, bumpy place I was in with Melissa. Lorna showed me in her own way how it is possible to drop even multi-generational patterns of disturbance.

I happily experienced Melissa open-up to me when I stopped judging her. A few months after my time with Lorna, Melissa invited me to work with her professionally. She had worked as an attorney for the Attorney General's office for the State of Washington for more than five years. She now had decided to become a life coach. Melissa achieved her coaching credentials in record time and loved working deeply with people. We both were interested in learning more about ancestral healing, and Melissa invited me to travel with her to Philly and NYC for some professional training intensives with an expert in the subject. The ancestral healing facilitator did individual sessions with each of us and remarked about how lucky we were to have achieved this intimate, respectful relationship. We knew he was right, and we were over-the-moon grateful.

We spent time with Melissa's sister Ally in Philly, where she lives. Looking back, that weekend stands out as one of the best in my life. Melissa and I shared confidences, and the walls between us dropped even more than I thought possible. I did not have the words for it at the time, but both Melissa and I were living from our True "I." Food and weight were no longer exceptions to our happiness. Our happiness was not linked to anything external.

Melissa made her own connections with her True "I." I do not know her exact process; I assume it was much like Gem's and mine. I do know the result was that she was open to love, open to more fun in her life, and filled with a new generosity. She began hearing messages like, *You will no longer have a need for money, so you can work for free* and *Buy this dress in size 14 to give to the person who will clean your room when you go to X hotel.* Melissa was connected to her True "I" in a way that freed her. Her worth was no longer in question. She saw herself as a vehicle of love in the world.

We got one last holiday with Melissa. It was perfect because Melissa loved Christmas. We tended to keep up traditions for her, because she was attached to our family's ways. That Christmas we explored a fantastic new creative American restaurant, for just the two of us. We giggled as we figured out with the maître de what ingredient could possibly make cooked carrots extraordinary. Less than a month later on January 23, 2018, we got a call no parent thought was possible: Melissa was dead at the age of 39.

Melissa had some confusing health issues, but none that had ever appeared life-threatening. The shock and devastation of her sudden loss created tsunami-level waves in my life and in the lives of all who loved Melissa.

I was texting with her on the last day she was alive. At the end of the fable, Gem gives advice to her mom. On Melissa's last day on earth, she texted me these words: "Mom, shine with your full brilliance, no matter what."

Shock and a kind of disbelief set in first. *How could we be in such a great place and then lose it all?* In some way, Melissa and I were so resolved, it was easier to let her go than if we had been stuck with unfinished business. After the disbelief wore off, I fought Melissa's death with looping thoughts like, *I don't think I can live with this pain. I miss Melissa so much; I feel deadened myself. Oh God, she was alone when she died. We'll never chat on the phone again, and I won't hear her miraculous observations again. No more lunches, vacations, meetings at Starbucks.* The looping thoughts and feelings that were on replay could go on and on, as I sank down into pain.

In those first months, it was like someone socked me in the stomach, but forgot to withdraw the punch. One morning, while walking on the beach near our Florida home, I imagined Melissa residing somewhere in the endless sky. I felt an invitation from the horizon to walk out into the ocean and just keep walking.

What stopped me from walking into the ocean? I noticed the suicidal thought, I acknowledged it was an unusual, surprising thought for me, but I didn't get upset, didn't touch the thought or follow-up the hurtful thought by adding on to it. And the impulse passed, replaced by thoughts of the sand and salt water beneath my feet. Having a direct experience with a powerful thought like taking my life and not needing to follow or add to that thought gave me the experiential knowledge of what Wisdom taught Gem in the fable. *At that time in my life, I had not yet been given the protocol the way Gem learns it in the fable: do not touch or add to hurtful thoughts.* Luckily, I didn't engage with the first thought and a different thought and feeling appeared within ninety seconds, exactly the way Wisdom describes what is possible to Gem.

One afternoon in late March 2019, I was sitting on a piece of driftwood at the beach. The ocean offered me compelling sounds with the crashing of waves. While I was mesmerized watching the dancing water, I felt Melissa's loss as I would a body flu ache with high fever.

Suddenly, someone was shaking me. But I was alone! It was like I was startled awake from a troubled sleep. A deep calm settled over me. Thinking was silenced. Emotions quieted. The shaking was definitely not internal, like nervousness, or quivering. The experience was as if somebody had taken me by the shoulders and pushed me brusquely back and forth again and again. I briefly questioned what could possibly be shaking me and why, but mostly I did not care who or what was shaking me. I began to again notice the ocean's private performance for me.

Nothing had changed. Melissa was still gone. But I noticed my aching, heavy heart was lifted. I could still remember suffering. But if I was honest, Melissa's "death" was no longer hurting me. How could this be? Where had the hurt gone? Wasn't I expected to suffer, if I loved my daughter? How many quotes had I heard like, "The degree of our suffering in grief is the degree to which we loved our person." I did love her before, and I do love her now. Where had the suffering gone? The difference from suffering to okayness seemed to be related to me not engaging with the temptations from thoughts and feelings. I was frankly stunned to feel okay, because I had felt so mercurial and okayness hadn't been one of my emotions since Melissa died. It was like a migraine was gone, and now I felt exhilarated. I did not have the concept of the True "I" at that time. But, if that language was in my vocabulary, I might have said I had regained my connection to my True "I." Of course, we can never lose the True "I." It can only be covered up by our diverted interest.

Since the shaking, I've had experience coming back again and again to my True "I." My homebase is never in question. I may step out and spend moments in thoughts and feelings, but it doesn't feel like home. I no longer have to go looking for my True "I" because presence in the Now is my homebase. Like Gem, I have felt more lighthearted, free and energized to connect with the world, since finding my homebase in my True "I."

Is suffering optional? Feelings can still hurt. Life can offer punches. But I know we do not need to make a home in places that hurt.

The True "I" belongs to all of us. It is our destiny to connect with this loving life force. May Wisdom find you!

Q & A WITH THE AUTHOR
ROSALYN ROURKE

Q1: The fable is a really sweet story. But in real life, don't we need to practice to get the results Gem experienced?

A: It depends on what you mean by practicing. Many seekers practice meditation, spiritual disciplines, affirmations or mind-set strategies to be a better person or fix their personality. Practices that are meant to improve our worth or our perception of our worth are not needed. When we find our True "I" our worth is not in question. We do practice noticing when we are having unworthy or hurtful thoughts. Over time, our observer develops a keen ability to catch hurtful thoughts that lead to suffering. Not interacting with the hurtful thoughts brings immediate joy and closes the door to additional suffering. We are using our observer in a way that helps us be with "what is." Freedom is in the Now.

Q2: Don't we all need improving?

A: We have been conditioned to believe we need fixing. By focusing on our thoughts, feelings and behaviors, we believe we will be fixed and worthy. When we focus on thoughts and feelings (the personality mind), we tend to idolize them, meaning we give them respect and value, even if the thoughts are hurtful. The True "I" needs no improvement. It's an energy that has never left us, that can be trusted to guide us because it is non-judgmental and 100% serves life.

Q3: When I hear there is a True "I" that has always been in me, with me, I don't believe it. I feel alone.

A: We have been taught that we can find our Self, the True "I," when we seek, find and achieve some imagined future goal. We can't feel our connection to our True "I" when we are busy trying to find ways to improve ourselves for the future. Connection is in the Now. Loneliness is sometimes directly related to Imagined Unworthiness.

Q4: Isn't it hard to change conditioning and beliefs?

A: When we believe in a conditioned thought, we will not have a desire to change that thought. Once we know conditioning does not equal truth, it becomes easier to spot the conditioned thoughts that are hurtful. For example, we are conditioned to believe the sun rises and sets even though we are taught that the earth moves, not the sun. Because of our conditioning, we sometimes talk about a beautiful sunrise and sunset. Because we *believe* our conditioned thoughts about sunrises and sunsets, we have no interest in changing them. Let's imagine, however, I have a realization that my false beliefs and looping thoughts about sunrises and sunsets are somehow hurting me. Instead of continuing to allow my looping thoughts to hurt me, now every time I think about the sun's rising and setting, I notice the false belief and say to myself, *Oh, that's a lie.* Once I identify the lie, I will naturally stop adding on and creating looping, repetitive suffering. If we got inside most people's individual minds, we would, I think, be amazed at how many hurtful thoughts and feelings pass as a normal day's experience. In Gem's situation, she had a realization that her attack thoughts about her body size were hurtful lies toward herself. It was a wake-up call to stop and not touch that pattern of thought and feeling.

Q5: Do I need to stop having negative thoughts and feelings in order to have the experience of freedom?

A: Negative thoughts are not the problem. It's adding to them that creates a story—and that's what buries us. Though I understand what you mean when you say negative thoughts, it's helpful to stop categorizing our thoughts and feelings into good or bad, or positive or negative. Noticing hurtful thoughts is different from judging or categorizing them. Once we sort them into positive and negative, we are engaged. I suggest you make friends with all your feelings and thoughts, because they are all just energy in motion. When you resist certain ones because you are calling them negative, you will be wasting your vital life force on a tug-of-war. In resistance, we are pulled into our imaginations and begin past and future looping, taking us out of the Now, where freedom is present.

Q6: Can't I fix my thoughts and feelings so that they do not hurt?

A: The personality mind seeks to find and fix perceived mistakes, things to worry about, imagined unworthiness or places or people to blame. When we try to fix ourselves and our thoughts, we are actually adding on to the hurtful thoughts. We are doing exactly the opposite of the protocol which is, *If it is hurtful, don't touch it.* By noticing and not touching the hurtful thoughts we are automatically creating some distance from those thoughts. That distance becomes very helpful by creating space for the True "I" to make its presence known. The True "I" has no agenda, except to be and fulfill our unique expression of life. It is such a relief to experience the cessation of seeking improvement, when our True "I" becomes our home base.

Q7: How do we go from reacting to thoughts and feelings to simply noticing hurtful and neutral thoughts?

A: Instead of fighting our reactivity, how about employing our observer? Just in noticing our reactivity, space is created. The next moment serves as a pause. If in the pause, you still find yourself reactive, notice that and start again. The space provided by our observer eventually feels like benevolent neutrality. Our observer calms our reactivity by giving us space from our typical reaction. When we add to our hurtful thoughts and feelings instead of taking the pause, we energize the hurt that keeps the cycle of reactivity going.

Q8: How do I know if my thought or feeling is coming from my personality mind, or my True "I"?

A: If you are agitated or upset, the personality mind is likely in charge and self-judgment or a fight with "what is" is likely involved. The True "I" nudges us toward actions and reactions, but there is never a judgment of self, or anyone else involved. The language of the nudge from the True "I" is impersonal. It sounds or feels like, *Move in this direction* or *Say yes or no.* When we say yes to the direction of the nudge, we're in acceptance. Acceptance does not mean we like the way life is happening. Instead, it means we have not picked up the rope in a tug-of-war. Acceptance of "what is" may be what released me from suffering after my daughter unexpectedly died.

Q9: How do I learn to accept "what is"?

A: When we are attached to the personality mind's ideas, we are motivated with thoughts and feelings of discontent with "what is." We may want to get more, change our circumstances or fix and change ourselves and those around us. When we're out of acceptance of "what is" and into fixing and changing life, we're in a fight with life. We are usually trying to change "what is" coming in the future or what has happened in the past. The Now is where acceptance lies. Groundedness, okayness and joy are present only in the Now. We get there first with noticing whether we are fighting "what is." When I was suffering after Melissa died, I was filled with thoughts and feelings that our family's future was unacceptable without Melissa alive. I also hurt myself with memories of happy past interactions like our wonderful conversations, which we would no longer have together. Now, if I begin to think about one of those wonderful memories, I notice that my thinking will lead to my suffering, because I can no longer have the ending I remember. Instead, I wake myself up to this moment and experience "what is" Now. Today, I value my freedom and openness above my feelings of nostalgia that for me have ended up in suffering. I can, however, remember a simple fact, like Melissa loved dogs, because then I am not trying to recapture a time that is no longer possible for me to experience with her in the world. I am not cutting off the memory of Melissa, I am cutting off my hurtful thought about her, because I do not wish to suffer and close down. I enjoy the widened, opened exuberance for living with inspiration from Melissa.

Presence in the Now, without the tug-of-war, brings a natural acceptance. Fighting "what is" has been a learned behavior. We have a false belief that fighting helps. If I scrape my knee because I tripped, attending to my knee scrape would be a direct acceptance. If I go to, *Who left the floor* wet or *I am so clumsy,* etc., I am adding psychological suffering to my hurting knee. It sounds too simple, but staying with "what is" without the fight leaves a space where acceptance of "what is" becomes a powerful starting place for "what is" next.

Q10: But don't we need to fight things like racial injustice and childhood poverty?

A: If we are led to take an action through the True "I," we will know it. Fighting might not be the best way to support children or a group being marginalized. Let's remember that there is not just one belief that we all agree upon, even about the word justice. If we judge the other, we are less likely to have an influence, or help the persons we are attempting to support.

Guidance from the True "I" might sound like, *Make calls to support that candidate who stands for racial justice.* Or, *Give money to this children's organization.* Or, *Organize a fundraiser for schools without technology assistance.* Not everyone hears their nudges in words. If you feel an inclination to help, check out whether there is a physical movement toward the action that is coming from deep inside you. Or is there a thought or feeling of *I should* motivating you? If *I should* is the motivation, that nudge is coming from the personality mind.

Q11: What if I don't know where the idea is coming from?

A: Then do nothing and notice what happens next. The True "I" does not deal in the past or future. It lives in the Now. If you are in either the past or future with your current thoughts or feelings, you can know you are not in the True "I." The past and future thoughts and feelings are imaginings that come from the personality mind. If the idea is from the True "I," it will have the ring of impersonal or neutral benevolence, even if the action is for you to express a big *no*. Sometimes the True "I" has us do something that is a stretch from our past behavioral patterns. The True "I" gives simple instructions like do this, say this, or be kind. If things are muddied with complicated feelings and motivations, it is best to assume it is not the True "I." Just await further instruction.

Q12: But what about the Stages of Grief? Don't we need to be involved with those feelings in order to get to Acceptance?

A: There is a mistaken idea that if we plunge into the feelings listed in the Stages of Grief, we will get to Acceptance sooner. In my experience working with people in grief as a psychotherapist for more than 30 years, Acceptance comes when we stop fighting "what is" or what has happened.

Most everyone needs to experience Shock after the death of a loved one. Shock is physiological, and it takes what it takes to reconfigure our lives, after a loss. If we were to go directly to Acceptance of "what is" after the Shock, we might not need to struggle with Denial, Anger, Bargaining and Depression. With death, we are often struggling with our emotions in a fight with what cannot be changed. Our security and peace come from living in the Now with acceptance and the grounding that it brings us.

Q13: If it is not necessary, why would people stay in these feeling Stages of Grief?

A: It seems that people sometimes feel they should feel pain because they believe that their suffering is a symbol of their love. When a relationship has been interrupted because of death, the relationship can feel incomplete in terms of unfinished emotional business. Those left behind may blame themselves for what was incomplete and struggle with thoughts of, *If I had only said or did x, y or z.* Suffering can feel appropriate, because it corresponds to our hurt. Western culture does not provide mourning rituals of expansion. There are expectations for us to contract, or close down with the emotions listed in the Stages of Grief. Instead, we could open or expand through our respect, admiration or love from and toward the person who has passed on. There is usually so much love around the grieving person. If we are open to allowing that love all the way in as a healing force, new life can seem to come out of the death. About two years after Melissa died, I began to hear a prompt from my True "I" to step into being an Inspirational Sunday Speaker for Jennifer Hadley's *Sundays With Spirit* for the first time. I felt a taboo-like feeling that I knew was Imagined Unworthiness. It was clear to me that the feeling of shame was because I was going against the rules of mourning. I didn't touch the feeling and soon I was filled with a knowing that I was living up to Melissa's directive to me in her last text: *Mom, shine with your full brilliance, no matter what!* I was living Melissa's inspiration by living larger instead of contracting into accepted grief behavior.

Q14: What helped you in your grief process, besides being shaken, to give you a realization of the expanded life that was possible?

A: Our family found that receiving love from far and wide for our loss, opened our family up in unimaginable ways. My old ways of keeping people at a distance disappeared. It felt like the boundaries between our family and other people were lifted when we cried together. When folks traveled to be with us at the beach house we rented, we had one of the most intimate group experiences of my life. We sprinkled Melissa's ashes and shared love stories about her. These close friends provided the strength to face the public memorial.

Q15: When you use the phrase "face the public memorial," it sounds like you were resisting that event.

A: We did notice resistance, which was a fear, but we did not change plans or worry, which would have been interacting with our thoughts and feelings about the memorial. Just noticing fear or resistance was enough to prevent a deep-dive into resistance. It turned out that by showing up to the public memorial with open hearts that had been well loved and nurtured at the beach by intimate friends, we again received more love than we ever thought possible. Melissa's coworkers spoke of her outstanding, brilliant service to the State of Washington. I will always remember the Native American Blanket Wrapping Ceremony when Allyson, our daughter, was caressed in a new blanket so that she could remember love whenever she felt the contraction of loss.

Q16: Can it really be that easy?

A: Yes, once we realize the nature of our investment in the thoughts and feelings of the mercurial personality mind, and instead make a home in our True "I," life can become quite easy. When we release our attachment to thoughts and feelings as though they are truth, we can look in the other direction for our True "I" for the constancy and peace for which we long.

Q17: Won't I be like a zombie if I don't interact with my feelings and thoughts?

A: Quite the opposite. Making contact with our True "I" is an enlivening experience. When we are no longer in inner conflict, but fully allowing life, we become more exuberant—we are more fun and have more fun.

Q18: Will the personality mind eventually stop offering up diversions from the True "I"?

A: Probably not, as long as our outer world still teaches success is from doing, achieving and having more physical goods. But when we become devoted to bringing the True "I" with us as our homebase, we don't mind that the personality mind continues to represent the teachings from the outer world.

Q19: In the fable and in the companion, you mention the Non-Dual method. What does Non-Duality actually mean?

A: Non-Dual means not two. Non-Duality informs us we are whole and an essential part of the whole. In contrast, Western culture teaches us that we are separate and thus either good or bad, right or wrong and so on. Within Non-Duality is a teaching called the Direct Path. The Direct path is derived from 8th-century Sanskrit. The Indian sage Atmananda Krishna Menon coined the phrase the Direct Path of Non-Duality to offer each of us the opportunity to experience freedom directly. Gem had her experience of the Direct Path when she stopped touching the looping thoughts and feelings and made space for the True "I" that was always within her. May you find your way to what is already within you!

BONUS MATERIALS

Find bonus materials and continued exchanges with me by visiting rosalynrourke.com

On the website, you will find

Meditations to guide you to connect with your "True I."

Front row passes for the book launch and book signing events in your city.

Up-to-date, behind-the-scenes details about book tour events and happenings.

Access to a free *When Wisdom Arrives* Book Club with me on Zoom.

An opportunity to take an Unworthiness Quiz and receive a written and video guide to my training: *Five Steps from Imagined Unworthiness to Living in Contentment Now.*

A gift of my story, *Tulip and Tree*, a fable revealing a different way to view death, loss, grief and causeless joy, plus admission to my free group: A New Paradigm for Grief.

A link to join me for a free Glimpses of Awakening Class where we'll apply the teachings from the book to your own life and find the opportunity of freedom now, in each of our lives.

ACKNOWLEDGMENTS

My heartfelt thanks to all the participants in my meetings, classes and audiences. You are what inspires me and deepens my knowledge and skills.

I need to thank my team of friends who are as young as 12 and as old as me. Each of you—Ann, Vivi, Coco, Lucy, Larisa, Rebecca, Jean Ann, Leigh, Patti, Susan and Jennifer—has had my back or helped in concrete ways with this book. You each know how valuable your specific support and/or editing have been to me and to this book's gestation and birth.

A special thank you to Katie and David for your significant collaboration and immeasurable assistance with developing and expanding the characters in this fable.

A huge thank you to Maureen, for making possible my meeting with Lorna Byrne, the Irish Mystic, who became the Wisdom intervention in my life.

To Rupert Spira and Byron Katie:

Byron Katie, you laid the groundwork for Loving What Is that made this book possible. Rupert, you first influenced my mind and then made sense out of my heartbreak after Melissa unexpectedly died. Both of you were collaborators in my transcending pain and suffering into a lived life of freedom.

To Mooji: Your Clarity has expanded my ability to live in Oneness. From years of listening to you, I've noticed your pointers live deeply inside me. When I have awakened in the night with any confusion from a dream or life issue, your voice has always lulled me back into clarity and somnolence.

To Jennifer Hadley: Thank you for standing with me in Truth when Melissa died. And when it was clear I was to start speaking and teaching, thank you for opening doors for my start.

To Bill Free: Your vulnerability and generosity have inspired me, particularly in your exploration of Non-Duality through your many venues. You have redefined A Course in Miracles with Non-Dual language, which was a gift to me and many others.

To Lisa Natoli: Thank you for being first my teacher and then my friend starting with A Course in Miracles and journeying together into Non-Duality. Your exuberance affects me deeply.

A shout out to Jenny Beal, who has been a powerful influence in my integration of Non-Duality into a practical form. There are many male presenters of Non-Dual teachings, but I have appreciated the wisdom and gentle presence that comes in your female way.

To Francie White: Without coming to your professional retreat, I might still be living with non-dieting as a concept rather than my own way of living. Thank you for offering me a teaching position and for the feedback you gave me, which I still use today.

To Geneen Roth: Without you, I might have stayed food-obsessed instead of living a full and rich life.

To Jane Hirschmann and Carol Munter: You blew my mind teaching me how bringing in copious amounts of forbidden food resolves any last food restrictions. Thank you deeply.

To Joyce Maynard: You inspired me to write about a beloved and then gave me my first lessons in how less is more with words.

To Adam Campbell: Our collaboration over the illustrations has been one of the great highlights of my life. Thank you for bringing Gem, Wisdom and Mom alive on the page.

To Mary Nelligan: Thank you for your brilliant and strong editing style. Through our intimate, trusting process, it became clear that this book is a memoir as much as a fable. Thank you for your dedication to the reader, to me and also to Melissa.

To Sara Connell, who makes books happen through joy, inspiration and mesmerizing leadership: Thank you for attracting a community of talented writers and editors who help sustain people like me.

To Charlie Mackesy: The drawings in your fable, *The Boy, the Mole, the Fox and the Horse*, captivated me and inspired the gestural style drawings in this book.

To Muse Literary and Patti Fors: Thank you for handling this book with tenderness. Muse is an author's dream, because they keep the writer's needs in focus.

ABOUT THE AUTHOR
ROSALYN ROURKE, M.S.W.

When Wisdom Arrives: From Imagined Unworthiness to Freedom is Rosalyn's first book. It is both a fable and a memoir. Unworthiness is another name for the feeling described as inner shame. Shame has not always been discussed as a psychological phenomenon. Rosalyn was one of the pioneers in the 1980's teaching shame as a phenomenon different from guilt. She graduated from Smith College School for Social Work in 1973 and has had a successful psychotherapy practice for more than 30 years. Rosalyn is a master Teacher and Coach of a personality system called the Enneagram. Her longtime experience with Non-Duality and A Course in Miracles helped make sense out of the unexpected death of her daughter Melissa at age 39. Rosalyn felt drawn to come out of a happy retirement to share her breakthroughs from suffering, shame and personality constriction to a life of equilibrium and stability. Rosalyn lives with her husband of 50 years in both Marco Island, Florida and Seattle, Washington. When she is not teaching or writing, she enjoys creating abstract art and spending time with her daughter, Ally, grandson, Ryan, and grand dog, Oaklee, a black micro doodle therapy dog.

ABOUT THE ILLUSTRATOR
ADAM CAMPBELL

Adam is an award-winning visual artist from Tulsa, Oklahoma. Illustrating *When Wisdom Arrives: From Imagined Unworthiness to Freedom* offered him the perfect opportunity to express his passion for sharing insight through art. He began illustrating publications for the School of Metaphysics in the early 2000s and graduated from the University of Arkansas in 2013 with a Bachelor of Arts. He enjoys walking the trails and watching the water flow in Northwest Arkansas, where he currently resides. More of his work is online at linktr.ee/creative_wave

Printed in the USA
CPSIA information can be obtained
at www.ICGtesting.com
LVHW010847080923
757555LV00007B/14